Stories and Storytelling

Norwegian Troll. One of the first written records of the use of the word "troll" is found in *Prose Edda*, a 13th century textbook about Norse mythology.

One Hundred Memorable Quotes About Stories and Storytelling

Compiled by

Ruth Stotter

Regent Press
Berkeley, California
2023

Copyright © 2023 by Ruth Stotter

ISBN 13: 978-1-58790-657-2

ISBN 10: 1-58790-657-0

Library of Congress Control Number: 2023939568

All photographs by the author

Cover: Moai, monolithic human figures carved on Easter Island (Rapa Nui) in eastern Polynesia between the years 1250 and 1500.

Manufactured in the U.S.A.
Berkeley, California
www.regentpress.net

Dedicated to storytellers, religious leaders, therapists, educators, librarians, and all who recognize the power of story.

Hopi Kachina warrior mouse. The traditional tale represented by this figure tells of his saving a village from a hawk devouring their chickens.

Open your mind and open your heart!

Storytelling is about to start!

~ 1 ~

The aim of art is to represent not the outward appearance of things, but their inward significance.

~ ARISTOTLE ~
[384 BC–322 BC]

Aristotle was an ancient Greek philosopher and a student of Socrates.

~ 2 ~

Telling stories is among the least costly and yet the most effective means of entertainment available to any family.

~ ANNE PELLOWSKI ~
[1933–2023]

Anne Pellowski is a former children's librarian for UNICEF, author of *The World of Storytelling*, and numerous additional publications related to storytelling.

~ 3 ~

There are just three essentials to a good story: humanity, a point, and the storyteller.

~ J. Frank Dobie ~
[1888–1964]

James Frank Dobie was an American folklorist, writer, and newspaper columnist.

~ 4 ~

There are three kinds of laughter. "Ha ha" laughter to amuse and entertain, "Ah ha" laughter for discovery of ideas and education, and "Ahhh" laughter, where the tales are sublime and connect the teller and the listener with a golden thread.

~ ARTHUR KOESTLER ~

[1905–1983]

> Storyteller Elizabeth Ellis (1943) uses "stories" and adds a fourth to his list: Ha ha, Ah ha, Ahh, and *AMEN*.

Arthur Koestler, Hungarian-born British novelist, journalist, and critic, is best known for his novel *Darkness at Noon*.

~ 5 ~

The purpose of the stories is to put an adult mind in a child's heart and a child's eye in an adult head.

~ Robert D. Pelton ~
[1935–2020]

Robert D. Pelton was a Roman Catholic priest, who pursued his studies in the History of Religions at the University of Chicago Divinity School. He taught West African religion and the meaning and practice of prayer at the University of Chicago.

~ 6 ~

A good storyteller stirs up the old words to make new soup.

~ Lynn Joseph ~
[1963 –]

Lynn Joseph is the author of numerous children's books.

~ 7 ~

In recent years, social scientists have come to appreciate what political, religious and military figures have long known; that stories (narratives, myths, or fables) constitute a uniquely powerful currency in human relationships.

~ HOWARD GARDNER ~
[1943 –   ]

Howard Gardner is a Developmental Psychologist and professor at the Harvard Graduate School of Education.

~ 8 ~

What really happens is that the story-maker proves a successful 'sub-creator'. He makes a Secondary World which your mind can enter. Inside it, what he relates is 'true', it accords with the laws of that world. You therefore believe it, while you are, as it were inside.

~ J. R. R. TOLKIEN ~

[1892–1973]

J. R. R. Tolkien was an English writer, poet, and philologist. Author of *The Hobbit* and *The Lord of the Rings* trilogy.

~ 9 ~

All sorrows can be borne if you put them into a story or tell a story about them.

~ Isak Dinesen ~
[1885–1962]

Isak Dinesen is the pen name for Baroness Karen Christenze von Blixen-Finecke, Danish author who wrote in Danish and English.

~ 10 ~

I am always at a loss to know how much to believe of my own stories.

~ WASHINGTON IRVING ~
[1783–1859]

Washington Irving was an author, historian and diplomat. Among his publications are *The Legend of Sleepy Hollow* and *Rip Van Winkle*.

~ 11 ~

He deserves Paradise who makes his companions laugh.

~ The Koran ~

~ 12 ~

Advanced middle age appears to be a popular time for admitting interest in fairy tales. At age fifty-five, George Bernard Shaw declared that he still considered "Grimm" to be the most entertaining of German authors. C. S. Lewis confessed to reading fairy tales on the sly for years; only after turning fifty did he feel free to acknowledge his addiction to the genre.

~ Maria Tatar ~

[1945 –   ]

Maria Magdalene Tatar is an American academic who researches and writes about children's literature, German literature, and Folklore.

~ 13 ~

If stories come to you, care for them. And learn to give them away when they are needed. Sometimes a person needs a story more than food to stay alive.

~ BARRY LOPEZ ~
[1945–2020]

Barry Lopez was an American author, essayist, nature writer, and fiction writer.

~ 14 ~

In my view the folktale is a narrative of adventures that represents in short form, sublimated and organized, the essential relations of human existence.

~ MAX LÜTHI ~
[1909–1991]

Max Lüthi, early scholar and author focusing on folktales.

~ 15 ~

Storytellers using narratives from other ethnic societies find it helpful to know something about their culture and worldview. Unlike anthropologists, storytellers do not study the story to learn about the culture. However, by studying the culture they learn about the story.

~ Ruth Stotter ~

[1936 –   ]

Ruth Stotter is a storyteller, educator, and author.

~ 16 ~

Aesthetic experience is a transference not only of feelings, but also of understanding.

~ ANANDA COOMARASWARMY ~
[1877–1947]

Ananda Coomaraswarmy was a folklorist, philosopher and largely responsible for introducing ancient Indian art to the West.

The future isn't here yet and you cannot foresee what it will bring. The present is only a moment and the past is one long story. Those who don't tell stories and don't hear stories live only for the moment, and that isn't enough.

~ Issac Bashevis Singer ~
[1903–2001]

I. B. Singer received the 1978 Nobel Prize for Literature.

~ 18 ~

When Sri Ramakrishna was asked, "Why, God being good, is there evil in the world?" answered, "To thicken the plot."

~ SRI RAMAKRISHNA ~
[1836–1886]

Sri Ramakrishna was a Hindu mystic and religious leader who proclaimed that the world's various religions are "so many paths to reach one and the same goal," thus validating the essential unity of religions.

~ 19 ~

... what the heart knows today the head will understand tomorrow.

~ JAMES STEPHENS ~
[1880–1950]

James Stephens was an Irish poet and author of *The Crock of Gold*, originally published in 1912.

~ 20 ~

As a narrative type, the folktale simultaneously entertains and illuminates the nature of existence.

~ MAX LÜTHI ~
[1909–1991]

Max Lüthi, early scholar and author focusing on folktales.

~ 21 ~

If the world were clear art would not exist. Art helps us pierce the opacity of the world.

~ Albert Camus ~
[1913–1960]

Albert Camus was a French philosopher, author and journalist who was awarded the 1957 Nobel Prize in Literature.

~ 22 ~

A story you hear is a letter that comes to you from yesterday. It passes through many hands and each one adds his postscript. "So it was with me, brother." And when you tell it you send a letter to tomorrow, "How is it there with you?"

~ GEORGE PAPASHVILY ~
[1898–1978]

George Papashvily was a Georgian-American writer and sculptor.

~ 23 ~

This feeling, an inexplicable renewal of enthusiasm after storytelling, is familiar to many people. It does not seem to matter greatly what the subject is, as long as the context is intimate and the story is told for its own sake, not forced to serve merely as the vehicle.

~ BARRY LOPEZ ~

[1945–2020]

Barry Holstun Lopez was an author, essayist, nature writer, and fiction writer .

~ 24 ~

**A grief shared is
half a grief.
A joy shared
is twice a joy.**

~ Irish proverb ~

~ 25 ~

Never trust the teller, trust the tale.

~ D. H. LAWRENCE ~
[1885–1930]

D. H. Lawrence was an English novelist and poet.

~ 26 ~

A lost coin is found by means of a penny candle; the deepest truth is found by means of a simple story.

~ ANTHONY DE MELLO ~
[1931–1983]

Anthony de Mello was a Jesuit priest and psychotherapist

~ 27 ~

Fiction is the lie through which we tell the truth.

~ ALBERT CAMUS ~
[1913–1960]

Albert Camus was French philosopher, author and journalist awarded the 1957 Nobel Prize in Literature. *The Myth of Sisyphus i*s one of his well know works.

~ 28 ~

At its best, when it's really working well, I feel like a conduit, connecting the old generations with the new.

~ SYD LIEBERMAN ~
[1944–2015]

Syd Lieberman, an Illinois storyteller, was often featured at the National Storytelling Festival in Jonesborough, Tennessee.

~ 29 ~

Kindness is the language which the deaf can hear and the blind can see.

~ CHRISTIAN NESTELL BOVEE ~
[ORIGINAL AUTHOR]
[1820–1904]

Since 1980 this quote has been attributed to Mark Twain. Mark Twain was the pen name of American author and humorist, Samuel Langhorne Clemens.

~ 30 ~

Stories are like fairy gold. The more you give away the more you have.

~ POLLY MCGUIRE ~

Polly McGuire was a San Francisco storyteller who founded the San Francisco branch of the National Storytelling Guild in the 1960s.

~ 31 ~

My vocation is to make extraordinary things ordinary, and ordinary things extraordinary.

~ KEN FEIT ~
[1940–1981]

After training as a Jesuit and serving as a Monk in Japan, Ken Feit spent his life performing, teaching and collecting folk tales. His business card read "Ken the fool, clown, sound poet, storyteller, puppeteer, mime, musician, and jester."

~ 32 ~

The *marchen* (Fairy tales) are like a kaleidoscope; the incidents (motifs) are the bits of colored glass. Shaken, they fall into a variety of attractive forms.

~ ANDREW LANG ~
[1844–1912]

Andrew Lang -Scottish folklorist, poet, novelist, literary critic, together with his wife, collected folk and fairy tales. They compiled and edited the *Lilac, Grey, Violet, Red, Orange, Yellow, Blue, Crimson, Green, Brown* and *Rainbow* fairytale collections.

~ 33 ~

Dream is personalized myth, myth is depersonalized dream; both myth and dream are symbolic.

~ JOSEPH CAMPBELL ~
[1904–1987]

Joseph Campbell was a Comparative Religions professor at Sara Lawrence University, author and editor. His works examined the universal functions of myth and mythic figures.

~ 34 ~

True art is supportive contemplation.

~ ANANDA COOMARASWARMY ~
[1887–1947]

Ananda Coomaraswarmy authored and lectured on folklore, literature, and visual art.

~ **35** ~

As a story is told,
the storyteller
inside each listener
sends up images
to meet the words.
A story is taken in
by matching the
words with scenes
instantly produced
in the imagination
of the listener.

~ Michael Meade ~
[1944 –   ]

Michael Meade is a storyteller, author and scholar of mythology, anthropology and psychology.

~ 36 ~

Fairytale force lies not in what meets the eye but in what dilates the heart.

~ JOSEPH CAMPBELL ~
[1904–1987]

Joseph Campbell was a comparative religions professor at Sara Lawrence University, author and editor. His works on comparative mythology examined the universal functions of myth and mythic figures.

~ 37 ~

Man is a storytelling animal.

~ SALMAN RUSHDIE ~

[1947 –   ]

Sir Ahmed Salman Rushdie CH FRSL is an Indian-born British-American novelist whose novels include magic realism and historical fiction.

~ 38 ~

Stories are Beings. You invite them to live with you. They'll teach you what they know in return for being a good host. When they're ready to move on they'll let you know. Then you pass them on to someone else.

~ CREE STORYTELLER ~

~ 39 ~

The narrative can be used to illustrate, to entertain, to introduce, and even to enlighten, because it provides those touchstones of recognition that give us the much needed sense that we are not alone on this journey.

~ MICHAEL PARENT ~
[1946–2023]

Michael Parent is a storyteller of French-Canadian descent who writes and performs in English and French.

~ 40 ~

When one listens to a story, one is being creative. The listener adds to it with his or her own imagination.

~ Arthur T. Allen ~
[1943–1971]

Arthur T. Allen is the author of "On Keeping the Sense of Wonder," *Fantasy for Children*, 1968. Vol. 69, issue 5.

~ 41 ~

To speak is to sow; to listen is to reap.

~ TURKISH PROVERB ~

~ 42 ~

Sharing stories of those we've lost is how we keep from really losing them.

~ Mitch Albom ~
[1958 –   ]

Mitch Albom is an author, playwright, and musician.

~ 43 ~

We can only tell stories truly, from the inside out. The outside of the story is simply its words - and why there should be so much fuss about the necessity of learning the words I do not understand. The hard thing is to understand a story from the inside.

~ JOHN HARREL ~
[1922–1996]

John Harrell was a poet, composer, musician, storyteller, and artist.

~ **44** ~

God created man because He loves stories.

~ Elie (Eliezer) Wiesel ~
[1928–2016]

Elie Wiesel was a Romanian-born American writer, professor, political activist, Nobel laureate, and Holocaust survivor.

~ 45 ~

To Navajos, a person's worth is determined by the stories and songs she or he knows, because it is by this knowledge that an individual is linked to the history of the entire group.

~ Luci Tapahonso ~

[1953 –   ]

Luci Tapahonso is a Navajo poet, writer and university lecturer.

~ 46 ~

A Zuni once asked the anthropologist, who was carefully writing down a story, "When I tell these stories, do you SEE it, or do you just
write it down?"

~ DENNIS TEDLOCK ~
[1939–2016]

Dennis Tedlock was a folklorist, anthropologist, author, and student of Mongolian shamanism.

~ 47 ~

The destiny of the world is determined less by the battles that are lost and won than by the stories it loves and believes in.

~ Harold Goddard ~
[1878–1950]

Harold Goddard was an English professor at Swarthmore College.

~ **48** ~

Every day of your life is a page of your history.

~ Arabic proverb ~

~ 49 ~

We all see our lives as stories it seems to me, and I am convinced that psychologists and sociologists and historians and so on would find it useful to acknowledge that.

~ KURT VONNEGUT ~
[1922–2007]

Kurt Vonnegut authored novels, short stories, plays, and nonfiction. He received the 1967 Guggenheim Fellowship award for Creative Arts, US & Canada.

~ 50 ~

The tapestry of life's story is woven with the threads of life's ties ever joining and breaking.

~ RABINDRANATH TAGORE ~
[1861–1941]

Rabindranath Tagore was a poet, writer, playwright, composer, philosopher, and social reformer. He received the Nobel prize for literature in 1913.

In the late 1880's Santiago Quintana began making Pueblo men with five children. In 1964 Helen Cordero (1915-1994) Cochito Pueblo) began making what she titled "storytelling figures." By 1982 there were 200 submissions at an annual folklife event by 50 different potters including Acoma, Jemez, Santa Clara, Zuni, Navajo, Tewa, Blackfoot. Hopi, and Blackfoot artists. The taller figure is signed Mary Magdalena, Jemez (that's the native affiliation). The shorter one is signed J. S. Shende, Jemez 1990.

Pegasus – In Greek mythology Pegasus is a winged horse, depicted here on an ancient Greek silver coin from Corinth.

This storyboard is from East Sepik, Papa New Guinea. Height 15"; Width 23". See *The Story of Storyboards from East Sepik New Guinea* by anthropologist, Martin Soukup.

Kavad – The paintings on this Kavad illustrate stories associated with Krishna, one of the most revered deities in Hinduism. For centuries traditional storytellers in Rajasthan have used the Kavad, commonly described as a portable shrine, as they narrate stories. The wooden cabinets have hinged doors which the teller flips back and forth while telling the story

Artist: Luccero (Jemez)

Telling stories on the street is traditional in many Arabic countries. Public performances by storytellers can occasionally still be found in Damascus, Fez, Cairo, and Bagdad. The storyteller depicted on this postcard (1911) is reciting from The Arabian Nights.

Chinese shadow puppets are made from animal skins such as cows, donkeys, goats, and horses. The puppets performances are frequently accompanied by music and/or singing. Manipulated between a light source and a translucent clothe so that they are illuminated from behind, their vibrant colors and movements can be seen by the audience.

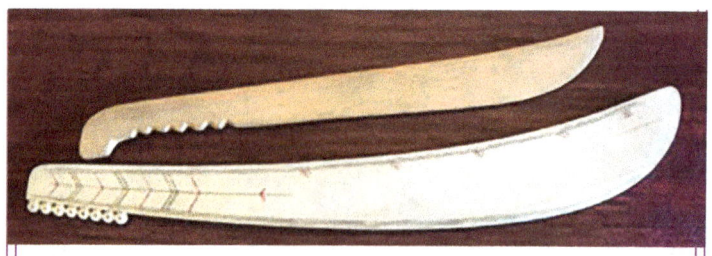

Ivory storyknife (1980) 15". Artist: Anthony Glazer.

Wooden storyknife 12". Artist: father of a school child in Scammon Bay, Alaska, 1980.

The storyknife is used by storytellers in SW Alaska to draw hieroglyphic figures in snow or mud. When a story changes scenes or characters the storyteller wipes away the images and draws a new one.

~ 51 ~

Talking is like playing on the harp: there is as much in laying the hands on the strings to stop their vibration as in twanging them to bring out the music.

~ OLIVER W. HOLMES SR. ~
[1809–1894]

Oliver Wendell Holmes Sr. was a medical doctor, professor, writer and member of the New England-based Fireside Poets. His son, Oliver Wendell Holmes Jr. (1841–1935) was an associate justice of the U.S. Supreme Court.

~ 52 ~

Imagination is more important than knowledge. For knowledge is limited, whereas imagination embraces the entire world, stimulating progress, giving birth to evolution.

~ ALBERT EINSTEIN ~
[1879–1955]

Albert Einstein, German-born physicist, developed the theories of relativity and won the Nobel Prize for Physics in 1921.

~ 53 ~

Art is communication, imitation, mediation, reorganization, re-creation, innovation, interpretation, reconciliation, and above all, celebration.

~ ADELE WISEMAN ~
[1928–1992]

Wiseman published plays, children's stories, essays, and other non-fiction. Her novel, *The Sacrifice* won the Governor General's Award, Canada's most prestigious literary prize

~ **54** ~

Give people a fact or an
idea and you enlighten
their mind.
Tell them a story
and you
touch their soul.

~ Hassidic proverb ~

~ 55 ~

Myths reveal their content to other levels of awareness than merely logical or reasoning mental processes; in some cases they leap beyond these processes to convey truth.

~ R. J. STEWART ~

[1949–]

R. J. Stewart is a Scottish-born composer, author and teacher who has published numerous books addressing Celtic mythology.

~ 56 ~

**The nymph Echo was punished by Hera who discovered Echo had entertained her with long stories so that she would not notice her husband, Zeus's, dalliances. Her punishment was that she could no longer tell her own stories;
Echo could only repeat what others said.**

~ GREEK MYTHOLOGY ~

~ 57 ~

All stories have this in common: they beckon us out of the visible, providing alternative lives, modes of possibility.

~ Paul Zweig ~
[1935–1984]

Paul Zweig was an author, poet and critic.

~ 58 ~

Storytelling is a personal art that makes public what is private and private what is public.

~ Jane Yolen ~
[1939–]

Jane Yolen is an American writer of fantasy, science fiction, and children's books.

~ 59 ~

The weeping of a hero is a feature which appears frequently in the world of the fairytale.

~ MAX LÜTHI ~

Max Lüthi, early scholar and author focusing on folktales.

~ 60 ~

**The tongue
is the rudder
of our ship.**

~ Arabic proverb ~

~ 61 ~

Fairy tales confirm, heal, compensate, counterbalance and criticize the dominating collective attitude, just as dreams confirm, heal, compensate, criticize and complete the conscious attitude of an individual.

~ MARIE-LOUISE VON FRANZ ~
[1915–1998]

Marie-Louise von Franz was a Jungian scholar and lecturer at the C.G. Jung Institute who authored numerous books exploring the relationship of fairy tales and psychology.

~ 62 ~

The folk tale is the primer of the picture language of the soul.

~ Joseph Campbell ~
[1904–1987]

Joseph Campbell was a Comparative Religions professor at Sara Lawrence University, author and editor. His works on comparative mythology examined the universal functions of myth and mythic figures.

~ 63 ~

In a fairy tale internal processes are externalized and become comprehensible as represented by the figures of the story and its events.

~ Bruno Bettleheim ~
[190–1990]

Bruno Bettleheim was an Austrian-born psychologist, scholar, and writer.

~ 64 ~

A performer of oral narratives utilizes materials of his or her culture much as a painter uses color.

~ HAROLD SCHEUB ~
[1931–2019]

Harold Scheub was a Folklorist who recorded and compiled oral literature from across southern Africa. He also authored *Story!* (University of Wisconsin Press, 1998.)

~ 65 ~

Storytelling can foster compassion – that miraculous ability to be disturbed by another being's misfortune, to feel joy about another being's happiness, to experience another's fate, as one's own.

~ KORNEI CHUKOVSKY ~
[1882–1969]

Kornei Chukovsky (real name Nikolay Vasilyevich) was a children's poet and author.

~ 66 ~

Fairytales address conflicts that continue to afflict individuals, families and countries such as cruel rulers and parents, sibling rivalry, and coping with challenging situations.

~ Ruth Stotter ~

[1936 –   ]

Ruth Stotter is an educator, folklorist, storyteller, and author.

~ 67 ~

Words have not just the astonishing capacity to banish boredom and create wonders. They also enable contact with the lives of others and with story worlds, arousing endless curiosity about ourselves and the places we inhabit. Such passion promises to keep us, at least intellectually, forever young

~ MARIA MAGDALENE TATAR ~

Maria Magdalene Tatar is an American academic who researches and writes about Children's Literature, German Literature, and Folklore.

~ 68 ~

**Sometimes the truth
doesn't fit, so I stretch it
and alter it
until it does fit.**

~ HERB GARDNER ~
[1935–2003]

Herb Gardner was a playwright and cartoonist.

~ 69 ~

As she retold her personal stories, Anna Quindlen *New York Times* columnist noted that details were refined, rearranged and "brightened like the ceiling of the Sistine Chapel after the dirt was taken off."

~ ANNA QUINDLEN ~

Anna Quindlen is an author, journalist and columnist.

~ 70 ~

No, it'll not do just to read the good old tales out of a book. You've got to tell'em to make'em go right.

~ RICHARD CHASE ~
[1904–1988]

Richard Thomas Chase was an American folklorist and author.

~ 71 ~

No two tellers present their tales in exactly the same way. Each new teller brings another perspective, another way of telling the tale.

~ MARGARET READ MACDONALD ~
[1940 –   ]

Margaret Read MacDonald is an American Storyteller, Folklorist, and author. A former librarian, she has published more than sixty-five books including picture books, books about storytelling, and the amazing *Storytellers Source Book: A Subject, Title, and Motif Index to Folklore Collections for Children*.

~ 72 ~

The motifs and themes of traditional folktales still permeate 20th century life. Names and concepts, such as the Golden Goose, Cinderella, Hansel and Gretel, Bluebeard, elicit emotional responses in us all, whether or not we know the "original" tales.

~ D. L. Ashliman ~
[1938 –   ]

D. L. Ashliman is a Folklorist professor. Her publications include the extraordinary *A Guide to Folktales in the English Language* and *Folk and Fairy Tales: A Handbook*.

~ 73 ~

To sum it all up, let us say of the method likely to bring success in telling stories, that it includes sympathy, grasp, spontaneity; one must appreciate the story, and know it; and then, using the realizing imagination as a constant vivifying force, and dominated by the mood of the story,
one must tell it with all one's might — simply, vitally, joyously

~ SARA CONE BRYANT ~

[1873–1956]

Sara Cone Bryant was an American lecturer and teacher who wrote children's books in the early 20th century.

~ 74 ~

God game us mouths that close and ears that don't. That must tell us something.

~ Anonymous ~

~ 75 ~

It would be a truism to suggest that dramatic instinct and dramatic power of expression are naturally the first essentials for success in the art of story-telling, and that, without these, no story-teller would go very far; but I maintain that, even with these gifts, no high standard of performance will be reached without certain other qualities, among the first of which I place apparent simplicity, which is really the art of concealing the art.

~ Marie L. Shedlock ~

[1854–1935]

Marie Louise Shedlock was an early and influential practitioner of the art of storytelling.

~ 76 ~

Thy loving smile will surely hail, the love-gift of a fairy tale.

~ Lewis Carrol ~
[1832-1898]

Lewis Carrol was an English author, poet and mathematician. Among his notable books are *Alice's Adventures in Wonderland* and its sequel *Through the Looking-Glass*.

~ 77 ~

David Reisman points out that storytellers are indispensable agents of socailiazation, and that, " Storytelling is like a handicraft industry; each telling is different from the other, and each is tailored to the taste and disposition of the audience."

~ DAVID RIESMAN ~
[1909–2002]
~ NATHAN GLAZER ~
[1923–2019]
AND
~ RUEL DENNEY ~
[1913–1995]

David Reisman (was an American sociologist, educator, and commentator on American society. Nathan Glazer was an American sociologist who taught at the University of California, Berkeley and Harvard University. Reuel Denney studied, analyzed and illuminated American popular culture as a scholar, author, teacher, journalist and poet.

~ 78 ~

I believe storytelling to be not only a folk-art but a living art; and by that I mean much. Music in all its forms is a living art in that it becomes a reality only when it is played. Dancing is a living art. for it lives only while you watch the movement, grace, interpretation of the dancer. So it is with storytelling; it lives only while the story is being told.

~ RUTH SAWYER ~

[1880–1970]

Ruth Sawyer was an American storyteller and writer. Her book *The Way of the Storyteller* remains a classic for storytellers.

~ 79 ~

No fairy tale should be interpreted or analyzed by looking at a single version.

~ JUDY SIERRA ~
[1945 –   ]

Judy Sierra is a former librarian and puppeteer, Folklorist, and author of numerous children's prize winning picture books.

~ 80 ~

When the old man died, the shell was lost. In time, the shrine, too, disappeared. All that remained was the story. But that is how it is with all of us; when we die, all that remains is the story.

~ DIANE WOLKSTEIN ~
[1942–2013]

Diane Wolkstein was New York City's official appointed storyteller. She authored numerous re-tellings of traditional folk tales, myths and legends.

~ 81 ~

When you make a story your own and tell it, the listener gets the story, plus your appreciation of it. It comes to him filtered through your own enjoyment. That is what makes the funny story thrice funnier on the lips of a jolly raconteur than in the pages of "Life." It is the filter of personality.

~ SARA CONE BRYANT ~

[1873–1956]

Sara Cone Bryant was an American lecturer, teacher, and writer. She wrote children's books in the early 20th century and took a leadership role in women's suffrage.

~ 82 ~

Dreams are the individual's folk-tales and folk-tales are collective dreams.

~ RICHARD ADAMS ~
[1920–2016]

Richard George Adams was an English novelist.

~ 83 ~

At the end of one of our storytelling residencies, one fifth-grader wrote: "I learned while telling my story in front of my class or other classes that they really didn't care how many mistakes I made. They just liked having me or anyone else tell them a story.

~ MARTHA HAMILTON ~
[1953 –]
~ MITCH WEISS ~
[1951 –]

Martha Hamilton is a former reference librarian, a professional storyteller and the co-author of numerous award winning books related to storytelling including *Children Tell Stories* and *Stories in My Pocket*.

Mitch Weiss, a professional storyteller, has co-authored with Martha Hamilton twenty-five books for young readers.

~ 84 ~

By definition variants of a tale share the same essential story, but the overriding emotional tone of a specific variant may be quite different from the next. A change in key from major to minor or a change in tempo not only changes the song, it changes what is shared. The same is true of folktales.

~ GEORGE SHANNON ~
[1961 –]

George Shannon is a storyteller, folklorist, and author of children's books.

~ 85 ~

But a story has to have two equal partners — tale teller and tale listener.

~ JANE YOLEN ~
[1949 –]

Jane Hyatt Yolen is an American writer of fantasy, science fiction, and children's books. She is the author or editor of more than 350 books!

~ 86 ~

Truth is stranger than fiction, because Fiction is obliged to stick to possibilities; Truth isn't.

~ MARK TWAIN ~
[1835–1920]

Mark Twain was the pen name of American author and humorist, Samuel Langhorne Clemens.

~ 87 ~

Some people think we're made of flesh and blood and bone. Scientists say we're made of atoms. But I think we're made of stories! When we die, that's what people remember, the stories of our lives and the stories that we told.

~ RUTH STOTTER ~

~ 88 ~

Art is the lie that reveals the truth.

~ JEAN COCTEAU ~
[1889–1963]

Jean Cocteau was a French poet, playwright, novelist, designer, filmmaker, visual artist, and critic

~ 89 ~

"We all have stories. Or perhaps it's because, as humans, we are already an assemblage of stories and the gulf that exists between us as people is that when we look at each other we might see faces, skin color, gender, race, or attitudes. But we don't see – we can't see the stories. And once we hear each other's stories, we realize the things we see as dividing us are all too often illusions; falsehoods. That the walls between us are, in truth, no thicker than scenery."

~ NEIL GAIMAN ~

[1960 –]

Neil Gaiman has authored numerous novels including *Norse Mythology* (2017), comic books, graphic novels, audio theatre and films. His novel *The Graveyard Book*, won the 2009 Newberry Medal.

~ 90 ~

Mythology is psychology, misread as cosmology, history and biography.

~ JOSEPH CAMPBELL ~

Joseph Campbell was a Comparative Religions professor at Sara Lawrence University, author and editor. His works on comparative mythology examined the universal functions of myth and mythic figures.

~ 91 ~

Fairy tales are the purest and simplest expression of collective unconscious psychic processes. They represent the archetypes in their simplest, barest and most concise form.

~ MARIE LOUISE VON FRANZ ~

Marie-Louise von Franz was a Jungian scholar and lecturer at the C.G. Jung Institute who authored numerous books exploring the relationship of fairy tales and psychology.

~ 92 ~

Paper is patient.

~ GERMAN-AMERICAN PROVERB ~

~ 93 ~

Great heroes need great sorrows and burdens, or half their greatness goes unnoticed. It is all part of the fairy tale.

~ PETER S. BEAGLE ~
[1939 –]

Peter S. Beagle is an American novelist who blends fantasy and realism.

~ 94 ~

A fairy tale princess's outer beauty is symbolic of her inner goodness. In real life, of course, a person who is beautiful on the inside can be all manner of ways on the outside. But that's not how it works in a fairy tale. The princess's beauty doesn't tell us that a person must be beautiful in order to be good. It's the opposite. Her inner goodness is represented by her outer beauty.

On-line post by
~ Faith Moore ~

Faith Moore is a stay-at-home mom and free-lance editor and writer

~ 95 ~

Remember folks: Story can become a verb just like wish, swim, and dance. Make time in your life for STORYING!

~ 96 ~

Tell me the facts and I'll learn. Tell me the truth and I'll believe. But tell me a story and it will live in my heart forever.

~ NATIVE AMERICAN PROVERB ~
(UNKNOWN TRIBAL SOURCE)

~ 97 ~

If I were a tree, each story I would tell would be like a new root growing deep into the ground – nurturing, nourishing and grounding me. What a gift a story is!

~ DIANNE MACINNES ~
[1960 –   ]

Dianne MacInnes is an educator, storyteller, and sculptor

~ 98 ~

Tell Me a Story

Tell me a story,
tell me a story,
Tell me a story,
remember what you said.
You promised me you
said you would.
You gotta give in
so I'll be good.
Tell me a story
then I'll go to bed.

"Tell Me a Story"
song written by
~ Terry Gilkyson ~

~ 99 ~

The wonderful thing about stories is that they present deep psychological and metaphysical truths, but in a poetic form which is gripping, beautiful, and entertaining.

~ DIANE WOLKSTEIN ~
[1942–2013]

Diane Wolkstein was New York City's official storyteller. She authored two dozen books retelling folk tales, myths and legends.

~ **100** ~

Story Water

A story is like water that
you heat for your bath.
It takes messages between
the fire and your skin.
It lets them meet, and it
cleans you!
Very few can sit down in
the middle of the fire
itself like a salamander
or Abraham. We need
intermediaries.
A feeling of fullness
comes, but usually it takes
some bread to bring it.
Beauty surrounds us, but
usually we need to be

walking in a garden to know it.

The body itself is a screen to shield and partially reveal to light that's blazing inside your presence.

Water, stories, the body, all the things we do, are mediums that hide and show what's hidden. Study them, and enjoy this being washed with a secret we sometimes know, and then not.

~ RŪMĪ, JALĀL AL-DĪN RŪMĪ ~
DATE OF DEATH: DECEMBER 17, 1273, KONYA [NOW IN TURKEY]).

Sufi mystic and poet.

EPILOGUE

And that's a true story.
If it isn't, it should be.

Is that story true?
It was true while
I was telling it.

And that's a true story.
If you don't believe me
give me a dollar.

Some folks say it
happened
and some folks say it
didn't.

And their wedding lasted nine days and nine nights, and if the last night was not better than the first, may the souls of my shoes turn to buttermilk. Irish

And I was there at their wedding. It lasted eight days and eight nights and each night was better than the one before, and I would be there still but I came here today to tell you the story.

If I get another story,
I'll stick it
behind your ears.
~ *Ghana* ~

There was a well and
in that well there
was a bell.
And that is all
I have to tell.
~ *Russian* ~

I left them happy
and home
I came.
May all your lives
be the same.
~ *Arabian* ~

And if they're not dead, they're living there still.

Index

Richard Adams - 82

Mitch Albom - 42

Arabic proverb – 48, 60, 74

Aristotle – 1

Arthur T. Allen – 40

D. L. Ashliman – 72

Peter S. Beagle - 93

Bruno Bettleheim – 63

Sara Cone Bryant – 73, 81

Joseph Campbell – 33, 36, 62, 90

Albert Camus – 21, 27

Lewis Carrol – 76

Richard Chase – 70

Kornei Chukovsky – 65

Jean Cocteau – 88

Ananda Coomaraswarmy – 16, 34

Cree Storyteller – 38

Anthony de Mello – 26

Isak Dinesen – 9

Ruel Denny – 77

J. Frank Dobie – 3

Albert Einstein – 52

Elizabeth Ellis – 4
Ken Feit – 31
Neil Gaiman - 89
Howard Gardner – 7
Herb Gardner – 68
German-American proverb – 92
Terry Gilkyson – 90
Nathan Glazer – 81
Harold Goddard – 47
Greek mythology – 56
Martha Hamilton – 83
John Harrel – 43
Hassidic proverb – 54
James Hillman – 51
Oliver W. Holmes Sr. – 51
George Howard – 67
Irish proverb – 24
Washington Irving – 10
Lynn Joseph – 6
Arthur Koestler – 4
The Koran – 11
Andrew Lang – 32
D.H. Lawrence – 25
Syd Lieberman – 28

Barry Lopez – 13, 23
Max Lüthi – 14, 20, 59
Margaret Read MacDonald – 91
Dianne MacInnes – 96
Polly McGuire – 30
Michael Meade – 35
Faith Moore – 94
George Papashvily – 22
Michael Parent – 39
Anne Pellowski – 2
Robert D. Pelton – 5
Anna Quindlen – 69
Sri Ramakrishna – 77
David Riesman – 77
Salmon Rushdie - 37
Rumi – 100
Ruth Sawyer – 78
Harold Scheub – 64
George Shannon – 84, 92
Marie L. Shedlock – 75
Judy Sierra – 79
Issac Bashevis Singer – 17
James Stephens – 19
R. J. Stewart – 55

Ruth Stotter – 15, 66, 87
Rabindranath Tagore – 50
Luci Tapahonso – 45
Maria Tatar – 12, 67
Dennis Tedlock – 46
J. R. R. Tolkien – 8
Turkish proverb – 41
Mark Twain – 29, 86
Marie-Louise von Franz – 61, 91
Kurt Vonnegut – 49
Mitch Weiss – 83
Elie (Eliezer) Wiesel – 44
Adele Wiseman – 53
Diane Wolkstein – 80, 99
Jane Yolen – 58, 85
Paul Zweig – 57

Sources

1. From *The Story of Philosophy: The Lives and Opinions of the Greater Philosophers* by Will Durant. Originally published, 1926.

2. *The Family Storytelling Handbook*, Anne Pellowski, Simon & Schuster, 1987, p.1.

3. "Obituary J. Frank Dobie," Stith Thompson, *Journal of American Folklore*, vol. 78, no. 307, January–March, 1965.

4. "Janus: A Summing Up", essay by Arthur Koestler, One 70 Press (1978)

5. *The Trickster in West Africa: A Study of Mythic Irony and Sacred Delight*, Robert D. Pelton, University of California Press, 1980. p. 279

6. *The Mermaid's Twin Sister: More Stories from Trinidad*, Lynn Joseph, Clarion Books, 1994. p. 29.

7. *Leading Minds: An Anatomy of Leadership*, Howard Gardner, Basic Books, 1995. p. 42

8. J.R.R. Tolkien (2012). *Tales from the Perilous Realm*, p. 351, Houghton Mifflin Harcourt.

9. From "Talk With Isak Dinesen," *New York Times,* Nov. 3, 1957.

10. *Tales of a Traveler,* Geoffrey Crayon, Daisy Tyler Modifie, 1824. This two-volume collection of essays and short stories was written by Washington Irving while he was living in Europe and published under Irving's pseudonym, Geoffrey Crayon.

11. Folklore archives

12. *The Hard Facts of the Grimm's Fairy Tales*, Maria Tatar, Princeton University Press, 1987, preface.

13. Spoken by the character Badger in *Crow and Weasel,* Barry Lopez, Century, 1990.

14. *The European Folktale: Form and Nature*, Max Lüthi; Indiana University Press, 1986.

15. *About Story: Writings on Stories and Storytelling.* Ruth Stotter. Stotter Press, 1994.

16. Coomeraswarmy

17. "Issac Singer: Writer for Children," Sylvia W. Patterson, *Children's Literature Association Quarterly*, Johns Hopkins University Press, 1981. p. 69–70.

18. Sri Ramakrishna. See *The Dance of Siva: Essays on Indian Art and Culture.*

19. *The Crock of Gold*, a mixture of philosophy and Irish Folklore, originally published by Macmillan in 1912.

20. *The European Folktale: Form and Nature*, Max Lüthi, Indiana University Press, 1986. p. 92.

21. *The Myth of Sisyphus and Other Essays*, Albert Camus, Alfred A. Knopf, 1961, first publication, Vintage Books, 1955.

22. *Yes and No Stories: A Book of Georgian Folk Tales*, George Papashvily and Helen Waite Papashvily, Harper & Brothers, 1946. p. 225.

23. *Vintage Lopez.* Barry Lopez; Penguin/Random House, 2004. p. 5.

24. Folklore archives

25. *Studies in Classic American Literature*, D. H. Lawrence, Cambridge University Press, 2003. p. 14. (First publication, Thomas Seltzer, 1923.)

26. *One Minute Wisdom*, Anthony de Mello, Image/Doubleday, 1985. p. 23.

27. Manuscript page in Camus' novel *The Stranger*.

28. Syd Lieberman

29. "Kindness. A language which the dumb can speak and the deaf can understand." was originally published in *Intuitions and Thoughts* by *Christian Nestell Bovee* (1962) and in a slightly different form in his earlier book *Thoughts, Feelings & Fancies* (1857). It has been attributed to Mark Twain since 2008.

30. From a conversation with storyteller and educator Ruth Stotter.

31. *Foolish Wisdom: Stories, Activities and Reflections*. Ken Feit, Resource Publications, 1990.

32. *The Grey Fairy Book* by Andrew Lang, 1900, p. v.11F. Originally published in 1900.

33. *The Hero with a Thousand Faces*, Joseph Campbell, Pantheon Books, 1949, chapter 1.

34. *The Dance of Shiva: Essays on Indian Art and Culture*, Ananda Coomaraswarmy, Rupa Publications 2013, first publication, The Sunwise Turn, 1918.

35. *Men and the Water of Life*, Michael Meade, Harper Collins, 1993. page 57.

36. Joseph Campbell, "Byos and Mythos," *The Flight of the Wild Gander: Explorations in the Mythological Dimensions*, Gateway Editions Ltd., 1958, p. 48.

37. From an online interview by Jennifer M. Brown. Random House Publishing Group published in *Self Awareness,* November 4, 2010, Issue 1323.

38. *Cree Narrative Memory*, Neal McLeod, Purich Publishing, 2007. Digitalized in 2010.

39. Michael Parent

40. From "The Ethos of the Teller of Tales," *Readings on Creativity and Imagination in Literature and Language*, L. V. Kosinski, ed., National Council of English Teachers, 1968.

41. Turkish quote

42. *For One More Day,* Mitch Albom, Hyperium, 2006.

43. *Origins and Early of Storytelling*, John Harrel, York House, 1983. p. 64.

44. From the preface to *Gates of the Forest*, Elie Wiesel, Penguin/Random House, 1964.

45. From *Culturefront Magazine*, Summer 1993.

46. From *Finding the Center: Narrative Poetry of the Zuni Indians*, Dennis Tedlock, Dial, 1972.

47. From *The Meaning of Shakespeare*, Harold Goddard, University of Chicago Press, 1951.

48. Folklore archives

49. From *Deadeye Dick*, Kurt Vonnegut, Dial Press, 1982. p. 235.

50. *Fireflies*, Rabindranath Tagore, Rupa & Co., Harper Collins 2002, first publication, Macmillan, 1928.

51. From *Autocrat of the Breakfast Table*, Oliver W. Holmes, Echo Library, 1858, first publication, *The Atlantic Monthly*, 1857.

52. Originally in "What Life Means to Einstein," *Saturday Evening Post*, October 26, 1929; reprinted in "On Science," in *Cosmic Religion,* 97.

53. From *Old Woman at Play,* Adele Wiseman, Clark, Irwin and Co. Ltd., 1978.

54. Folklore archives

55. From *The Elements of Creation Myths*, R. J. Stewart, Element Books, 1989.

56. Greek Mythology

57. *The Adventurer,* Paul Zweig, Basic Books, 1974. p. 83.

58. *Favorite Folktales From Around the World*, Jane Yolen, ed., Random House Inc., 1986. p. 13.

59. Max Luthi, *The Fairytale as Art Form and Portrait of Man* (translated by Jon Erickson) Indiana University Press,1984. Original publication by Eugene D. Verlag 1975. p. 8

60. Folklore archives

61. *Individuation in Fairy Tales*, Marie-Louise von Franz, Spring Publications, 1977, p. 124

.

62. *The Flight of the Gander: Explorations in the Mythological Dimension*, Joseph Campbell, Gateway Editions Ltd., 1958.

63. From *The Uses of Enchantment: The Meaning and Importance of Fairy Tales*, Bruno Bettelheim, Alfred A. Knopf, 1976.

64. Cultural Tales: A Narrative Approach to Thinking, Cross-Cultural Psychology and Psychotherapy," *American Psychologist*. p. 187-197,

65. *From Two to Five*. University of California, 1961.

66. Lecture note in Analyzing Fairytales seminar, 2023.

67. Enchanted Hunters: The power of stories in Childhood. Maria M. Tatar. W.W. Norton & Company, Inc., 2009. Introduction, p. 31.

68. From *I'm Not Rapoport*, Herb Gardner, a play on Broadway, 1985–1988.

69. The New York Times. October 27, 1988. Section C - Home and Gardens. p. 2.

70. *Grandfather Tales: American-English Folk Tales,* Richard Chase, Clarion Books, 2003, first publication, Houghton Mifflin, 1948.

71. *The Story-Teller's Start-Up Book: Finding, Learning, Performing and Using Folktales*, Margaret Read MacDonald, August House, 1993. p.11.

72. *A Guide to Folktales in the English Language*, D.L. Ashliman, Greenwood Press, 1987, p. xii.

73. *How to Tell Stories to Children*, Sara Cone Bryant, Houghton Mifflin Co., 1905, p. 109.

74. Folklore archives

75. *The Art of the Story-Teller*, Marie L. Shedlock, Dover Publications, 1951, p. 23.

76. From *Through the Looking-Glass and What Alice Found There*, Lewis Carrol (pen name for Charles Lutwidge Dodgson). First publication, 1871.

77. *The Lonely Crowd: A Study of the Changing American Character*, David Riesman, Nathan Glazer and Ruel Denney. Yale Uiniversity Press, 1950. p. 87.

78. *The Way of the Storyteller*, Ruth Sawyer, Viking Press 1942 and 1967, Penguin Books, 1977. p. 29.

79. *Quests and Spells*, Judy Sierra, Kaminski Media Arts, 1994. p. 171.

80. From *White Wave: A Chinese Tale*, Diane Wolkstein. Thomas Y. Crowell Co, 1979.

81. *How to Tell Stories to Children*, Sara Cone Bryant, Houghton Mifflin Co., 1905. p. xvi.

82. *The Unbroken Web*, Richard Adams, Crown Publishers, 1988.

83. *Teaching Children to Tell Stories*, Martha Hamilton and Mitch Weiss (2005).

84. *A Knock at the Door*, Oryx Multicultural Folktale Series, Oryx Press, 1992, p.viii.

85. *Touch Magic,* Jane Yolen, Philomel Books, 1951

86. *Following the Equator: A Journey Around the World,* Mark Twain, The American Publishing Co., Hartford, 1897.

87. From *The Storyteller's Calendar*, Ruth Stotter, Stotter Press, 1992.

88. Published in an article by Jean Cocteau, *Comoedia*, a literary and artistic periodical, p 2, col. 6, 1937

89. *The View From the Cheap Seats: Selected Nonfiction* - William Morrow Paperbacks, 2017.

90. *The Flight of the Wild Gander.* Joseph Campbell. Gateway Editions, 1951. p. 33.

91. *Interpretation of Fairytales.* Marie Louise Von Franz. Spring Publications. 1987, p. 1.

92. German-American Folklore compiled and edited by Mac E. Barrick. *A Living Legacy in Proverbs, Riddles, Crafts and More* (even recipes!) August House, Inc. 1987.

93. Quote posted on his website.

94. On-line post by Faith Moore: *Why Can't The Princess Be Ugly? Fairy Tale Symbolism and Why It Matters,* August 17, 2019.

95. Terry Gikyson

96. (unknown tribal source)

97. Conversation with storyteller Ruth Stotter

98. Rumi

99. Diane Wolkstein, conversations at National Storytelling Festival, Jonesborogh, TN, 1979.

100. Ruth Stotter

About the Compiler

Ruth Stotter has performed and taught storytelling on five continents. She was the director of the Dominican college Certificate-in-Storytelling program in San Rafael, California and is the author of numerous books related to Folklore and Storytelling. She received a Lifement Achievement Oracle Award from the National Storytelling Network, 2010.

www.ingramcontent.com/pod-product-compliance
Lightning Source LLC
Chambersburg PA
CBHW070146080526
44586CB00015B/1860